DRAW
Medieval Fantasies

by

Damon J. Reinagle

PEELproductions, inc.

For my wonderful and
supportive family. Thanks!

–DJR

Manufactured in the United States of America

Library of Congress Cataloging-in-Publication Data

Reinagle, Damon J.

Draw : medieval fantasies / by Damon J. Reinagle

p. cm.

Summary: Offers step-by-step instructions for drawing dragons,
castles, and other objects of the medieval world; covers basic skills
as well as advanced drawing techniques.

ISBN 0-939217-30-9

1. Dragons in art--Juvenile literature. 2. Castles in art--Juvenile
literature. 3. Heroes in art--Juvenile literature. 4. Villains in art--
Juvenile literature. 5. Drawing--Technique--Juvenile literature. [1.
Dragons in art. 2. Knights and knighthood in art. 3. Drawing--
Technique.] I. Title.

NC825.D72R45

743'.87--dc20   95-31190

Distributed to the trade and art
markets in North America by

NORTH LIGHT BOOKS,
an imprint of F&W Publications, Inc.
4700 East Galbraith Road
Cincinnati, OH 45236

(800) 289-0963

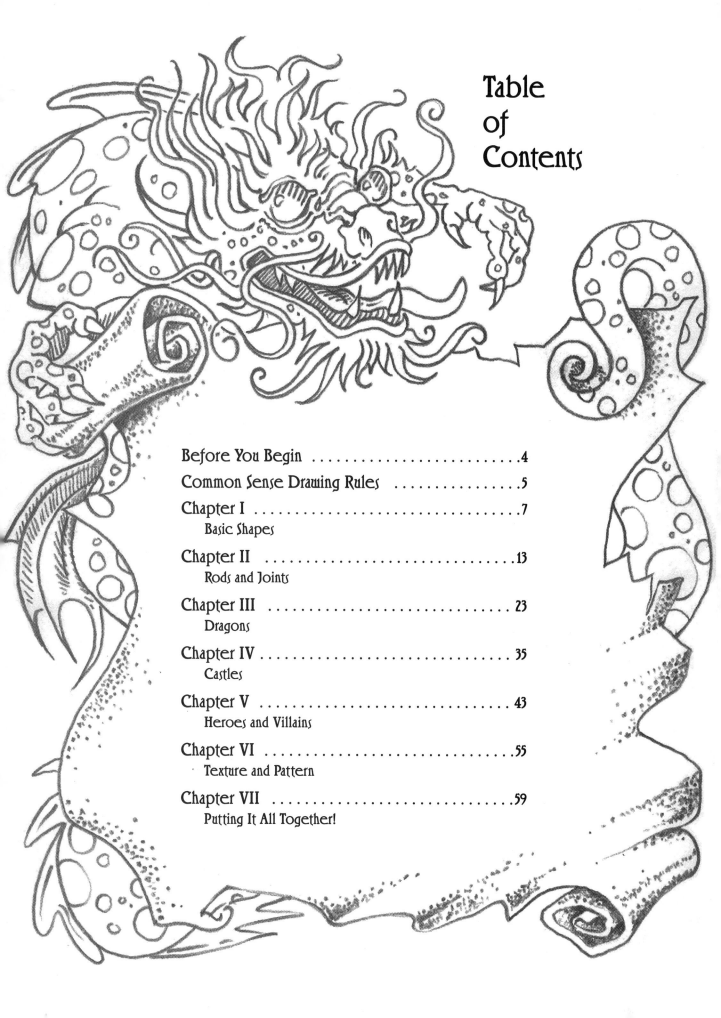

Table of Contents

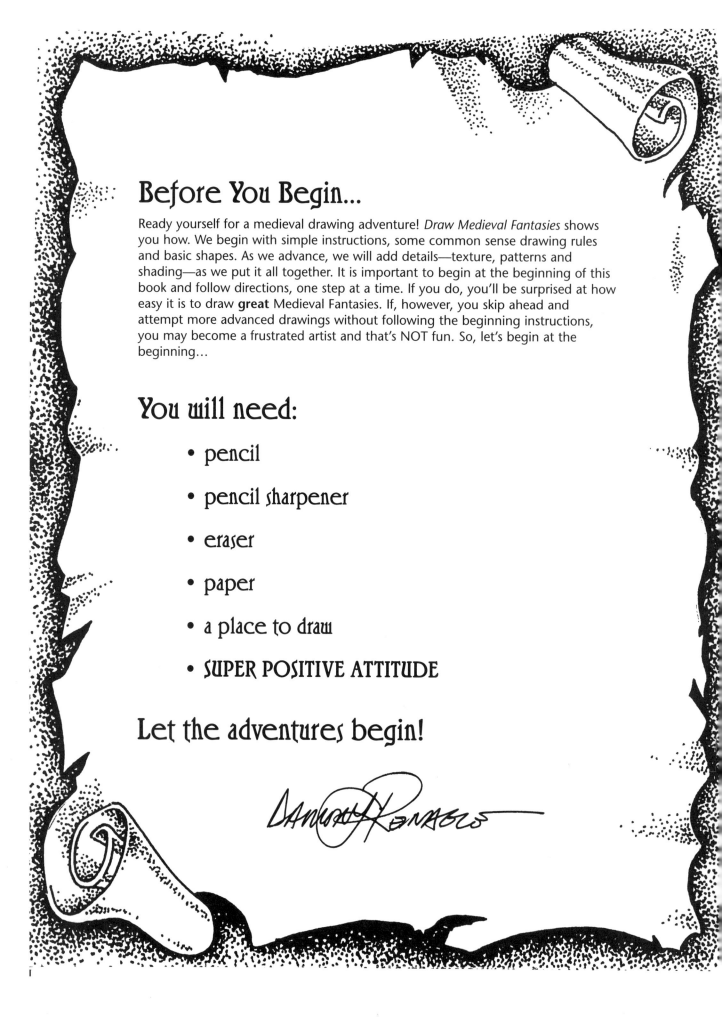

Before You Begin...

Ready yourself for a medieval drawing adventure! *Draw Medieval Fantasies* shows you how. We begin with simple instructions, some common sense drawing rules and basic shapes. As we advance, we will add details—texture, patterns and shading—as we put it all together. It is important to begin at the beginning of this book and follow directions, one step at a time. If you do, you'll be surprised at how easy it is to draw **great** Medieval Fantasies. If, however, you skip ahead and attempt more advanced drawings without following the beginning instructions, you may become a frustrated artist and that's NOT fun. So, let's begin at the beginning…

You will need:

- pencil
- pencil sharpener
- eraser
- paper
- a place to draw
- SUPER POSITIVE ATTITUDE

Let the adventures begin!

Common Sense Drawing Rules

Rule I

LOOK! See the shapes

Most everything you can draw is based on simple geometric shapes like circles, squares, rectangles and triangles. If you concentrate and observe, you can see shapes in everything you look at. LOOK! See the shapes

Rule II

Sketch super lightly—always, always, always!

Reconstructive surgery (erasing) is much easier if you sketch lightly. And, light sketch lines help create form and texture in shapes. So always, always, always sketch super lightly!

Rule III

Be Creative! Use your imagination.

You could become an expert at copying the step by step drawings in this book. But, the real satisfaction comes when you make up your own characters and fantasy worlds, from your imagination. So be creative! Use your imagination!

Rule IV

Practice, Practice, Practice!

If at first you don't succeed…Practice, practice, practice and you will get better.

All artists, beginners and professionals who follow these important drawing rules are guaranteed **GREAT** drawings!

Chapter I

Basic   Shapes

Tilting Ovals

Most everything that you draw can be based on simple geometric shapes like circles, ovals, squares, rectangles and triangles. Many drawings start with ovals.

See how this shield drawing starts with an oval?

However, the ovals don't always go straight up and down. More often, in drawings, they tilt.

As you study this book, you'll find many drawings that start with ovals. As you look at them, think of a clock face, and compare the tilt of the oval to the clock face.

The shield this knight holds is tilted. The tilt of the oval is a 1 o'clock—7 o'clock tilt. Tilting the shield makes the drawing more interesting than if the shield simply went straight up and down.

Aha! But notice the knight's head is also tilted!

How does the bottom of the visor line up on the clock face? The center of the visor?

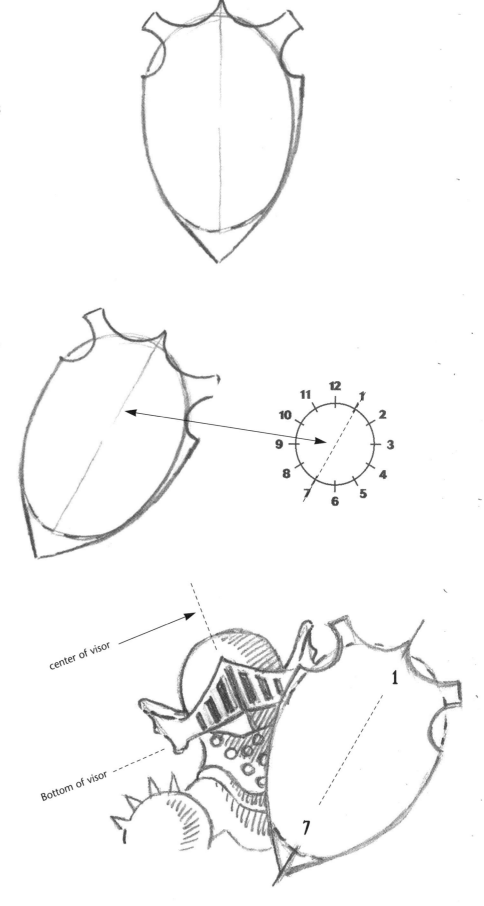

center of visor

Bottom of visor

1

7

Take some scrap paper and practice drawing circles and ovals. This will loosen up your hand and perfect your drawing skills.

Practice Every Day.

Practice will increase your ability and confidence. Draw circles and ovals of all sizes—fat, skinny, tall, squat—tilting every which way. Draw circles inside circles. Draw ovals inside ovals.

Practice, practice, practice, and you will get better.

Try some tilted so much that they look like swiss cheese holes.

Loosen up your hand, arm and imagination!

Something else that will loosen up and energize your drawings is the use of curved and jagged lines.

What could this jagged line be? Scales on the back of a dragon? Waves on a choppy sea?

How about this curved line?

A splash of paint?

A horse's mane?

Now, draw some squiggly, wiggly curved and jagged lines. Loosen up your hand, arm and imagination. Make them up as you go.

Draw some lines very slowly and controlled. Now, draw some as fast as you can. Have fun!

Here, you can see tilted ovals and curved lines in action. The knight's head starts with a tilted oval (what is the tilt, according to the clock face?). Other details are added, using curved lines for the helmet and plume.

Below, ovals within ovals and curved and jagged lines form the head of this charming character.

What is the tilt of the main oval?

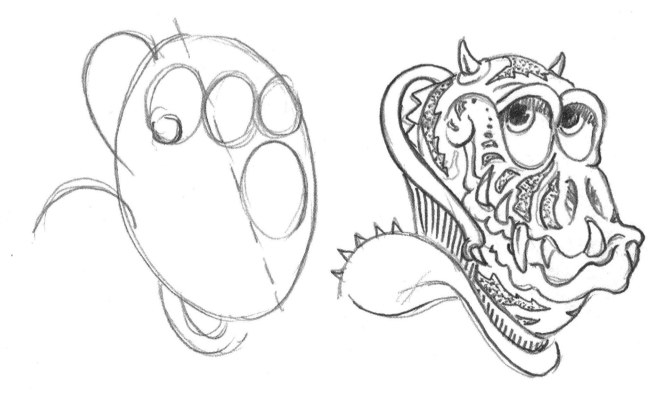

Let's draw!
Step by step...from a tilted oval

Step 1

Sketch a tilted oval. What's the tilt (look at the clock face)? Lightly sketch the tilt line.

Step 2

Add a triangle to the top of the oval and two eye lines.

Step 3

Draw a ridge under the triangle. Add a curved line, from top to bottom, as a guide line for the nose and mouth. Draw curved lines, on either side of the bottom eye line, to form the eye holes in the helmet.

Step 4

Sketch an oval and curved line as guide lines for the horns. Erase the tilt line. Add curved lines to shape the helmet.

Step 5

Draw additional lines for the helmet, horns and face. Erase guide lines.

Step 6

Finish horns. Draw more helmet lines. Add eyes and nose.

Step 7

Detail helmet. Draw jagged lines for fur. Add shading and other details you see.

Good job!

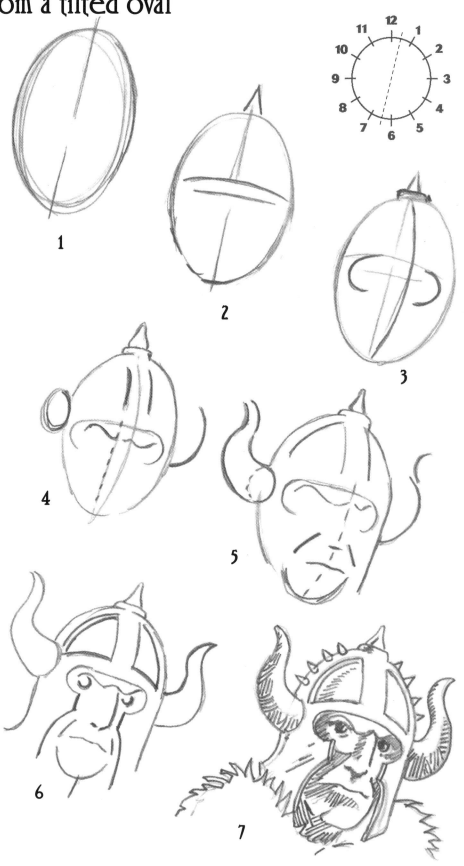

Chapter II

Rods and Joints

The Warrior

If we took away all the armor, clothing, skin and muscle from the warrior on the next page, we would see this skeleton.

But, it's much easier to draw the warrior using RODS (lines) and JOINTS (ovals), than to draw an entire skeleton!

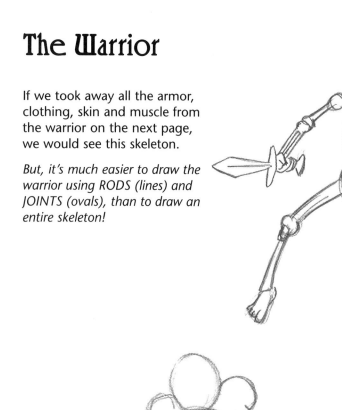

Step 1

First, look carefully at this figure made of ovals, rods and joints. Sketch ovals for the head, shoulders, body, pectorals (chest muscles), and hips. Add rods and joints for the arms and legs. Sketch lines for feet. Pay careful attention to the direction each line runs!

RODS (lines)

JOINTS (ovals)

Step 2

Sketch lines for facial features. Draw curved lines to shape the body and arms. Draw fingers and a handle for the weapon. Draw lines to shape legs and feet. Erase guide lines.

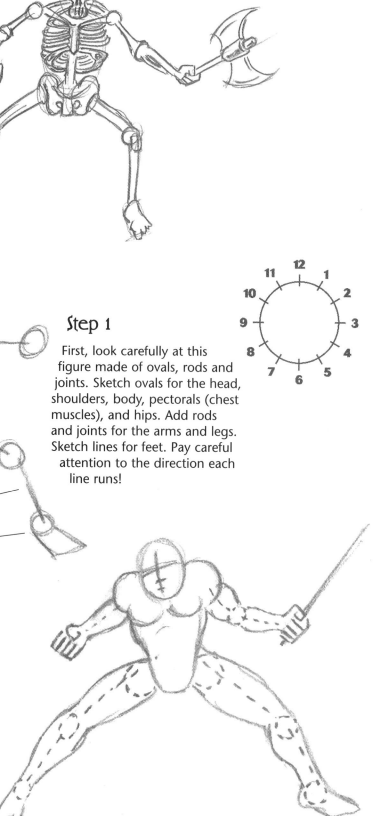

Step 3

Now, for the details:

You can make your warrior an axe welding male…

or…

add long flowing hair and round out the breasts for his female counterpart!

You decide.

Use your imagination!

Draw helmet, facial features, weapons, body suit, boots, and other details you see.

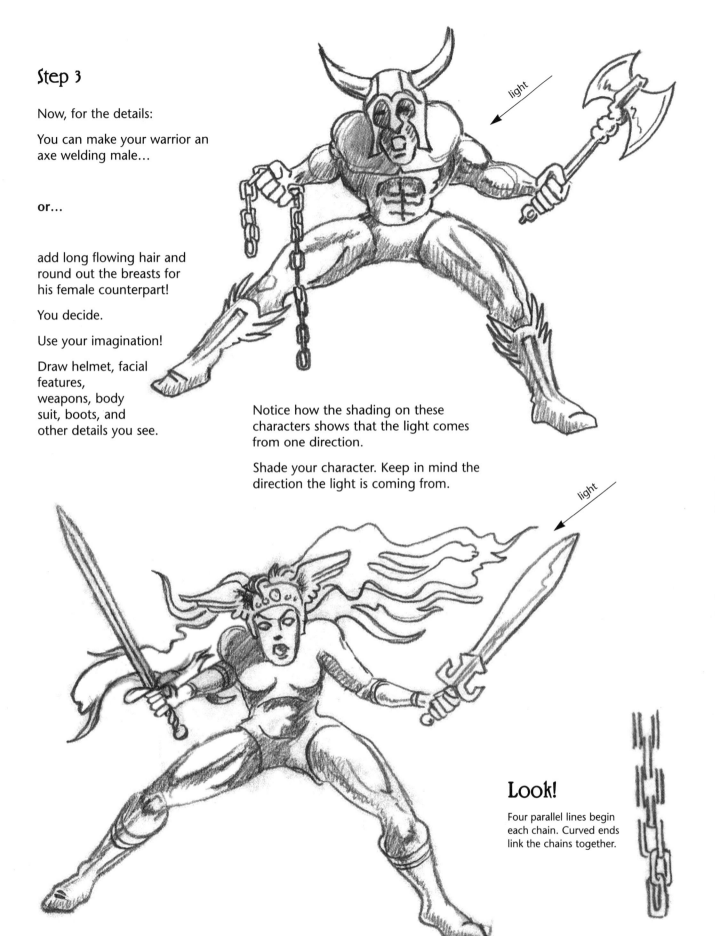

light

Notice how the shading on these characters shows that the light comes from one direction.

Shade your character. Keep in mind the direction the light is coming from.

light

Look!

Four parallel lines begin each chain. Curved ends link the chains together.

The Winged Unicorn

A basic horse body is made up of many ovals and lines.

Before you start this drawing, do some warm-up ovals and lines. Sketch lightly. Don't be afraid to overlap ovals and lines to get the feel of the animal's shape.

Step 1

Sketch ovals for the head and body. Draw lines connecting them to each other.

Look carefully at the clock face to establish the directions the legs will go. Draw rods (lines) and joints (ovals) to begin the legs.

Step 2

Sketch a triangular shape for the beginning of the horse's wing. Draw curved lines to connect the head to the body. Draw the horn. Draw lines to shape the legs. Draw a curving line for the tail.

Erase the rods and joints guide lines.

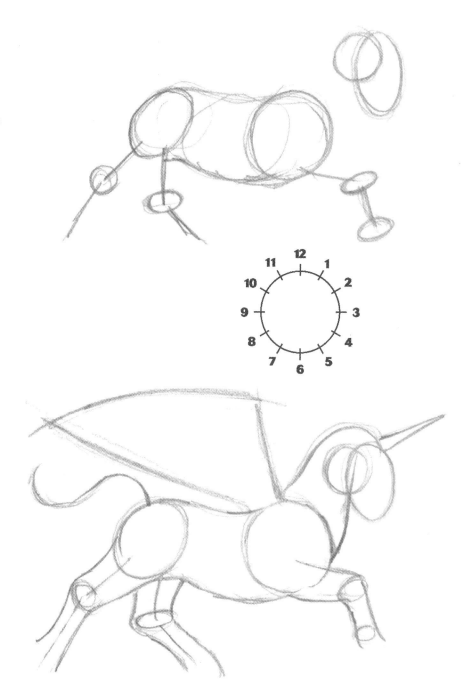

Remember...

KEEP A POSITIVE ATTITUDE!

Don't expect your drawings to look exactly like the ones in this book, the very first time you draw them. If at first you don't succeed...Practice, practice, practice and you will get better!

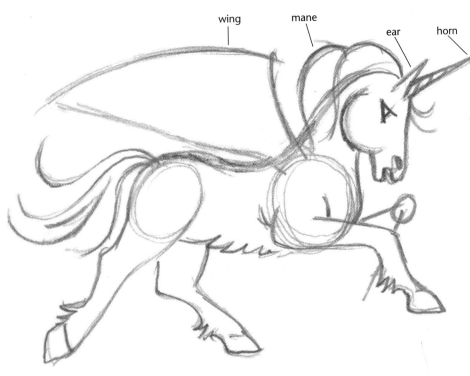

wing   mane   ear   horn

Step 3

Starting with the head, draw a triangle for the ear and one for the eye. Draw lines to shape the head, mouth and nostril. Draw curved lines for the mane, other wing and tail. Draw the three hooves. Draw jagged lines for shaggy hair—above the hooves and under the belly.

Lightly sketch the rods and joint for the other front leg.

Step 4

Draw lines to shape the other front leg and hoof. Erase rod and joint lines. Draw curved lines to divide the wings into feather shapes. Finish off the tail and the mane with additional flowing, curved lines. Detail the horn and face.

Erase lines you no longer need *(you did start out lightly, didn't you?)*.

Lizardman

Check out how real anatomy can be combined with fantasy detail to create a truly unique character. The Lizardman is a perfect example of a character you can draw starting with a simple geometric shape.

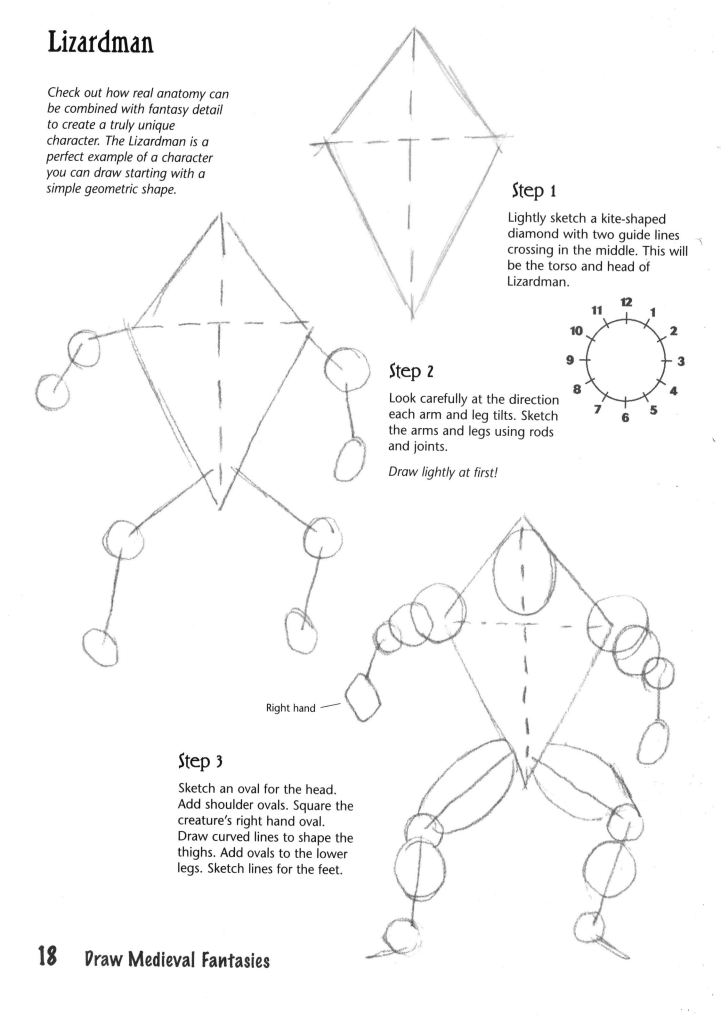

Step 1

Lightly sketch a kite-shaped diamond with two guide lines crossing in the middle. This will be the torso and head of Lizardman.

Step 2

Look carefully at the direction each arm and leg tilts. Sketch the arms and legs using rods and joints.

Draw lightly at first!

Right hand

Step 3

Sketch an oval for the head. Add shoulder ovals. Square the creature's right hand oval. Draw curved lines to shape the thighs. Add ovals to the lower legs. Sketch lines for the feet.

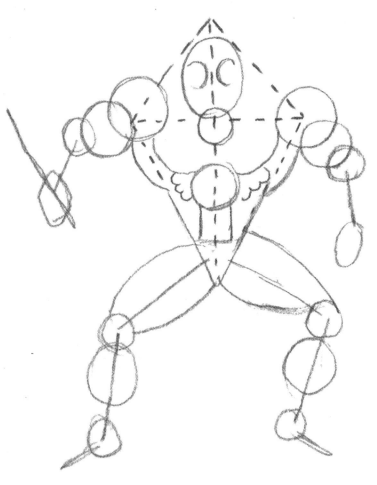

Step 4

Draw half ovals for eyes and a full oval for the mouth. Sketch an oval and a rectangle in the stomach area. Draw curved lines to outline the chest and stomach muscles.

Draw the shaft of the weapon—notice that it's at an angle.

Step 5

Draw jagged lines around the head for a hairy look. Detail the face. Draw curved lines to shape the shoulders. Draw shoulder spikes. Shape the arms, hands and fingers. Draw the weapon in his right hand.

Draw curved lines to shape the legs. Draw ovals for the toes.

Look carefully! Are there any details I've missed? Add them!

Erase guide lines.

Now for the details....

Here are two different approaches to finishing off a drawing.

light

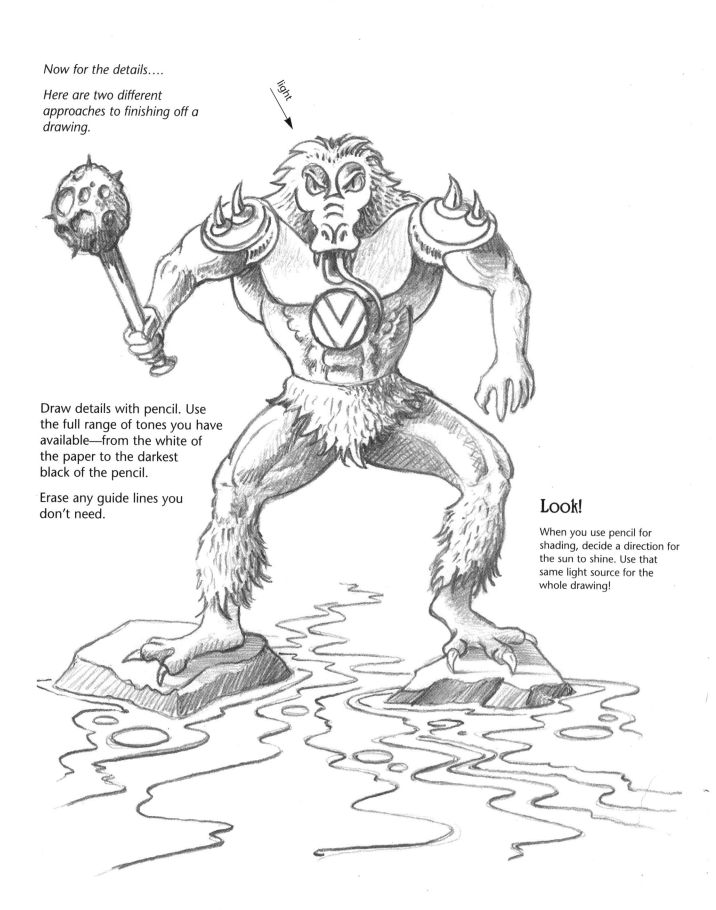

Draw details with pencil. Use the full range of tones you have available—from the white of the paper to the darkest black of the pencil.

Erase any guide lines you don't need.

Look!

When you use pencil for shading, decide a direction for the sun to shine. Use that same light source for the whole drawing!

Or...

You can draw a striking black and white masterpiece using a fine tip black marker. Finish off the background with fun, zigzag designs for texture!

When the drawing is finished, and the ink is dry, carefully erase the pencil guide lines.

Gesture Drawing

Gesture drawings are quick sketches, done with mostly curved lines and oval shapes. Most artists start out with these loose drawings before they spend the time working on a final drawing with details.

Notice that both of the knight sketches start with the same three basic ovals for the head and body. By changing the position of the knight's arms and legs, the characters take on totally different attitudes.

Look at the gesture drawings on this page. Try drawing some of these and then make up some of your own.

How about a jester gesture drawing?

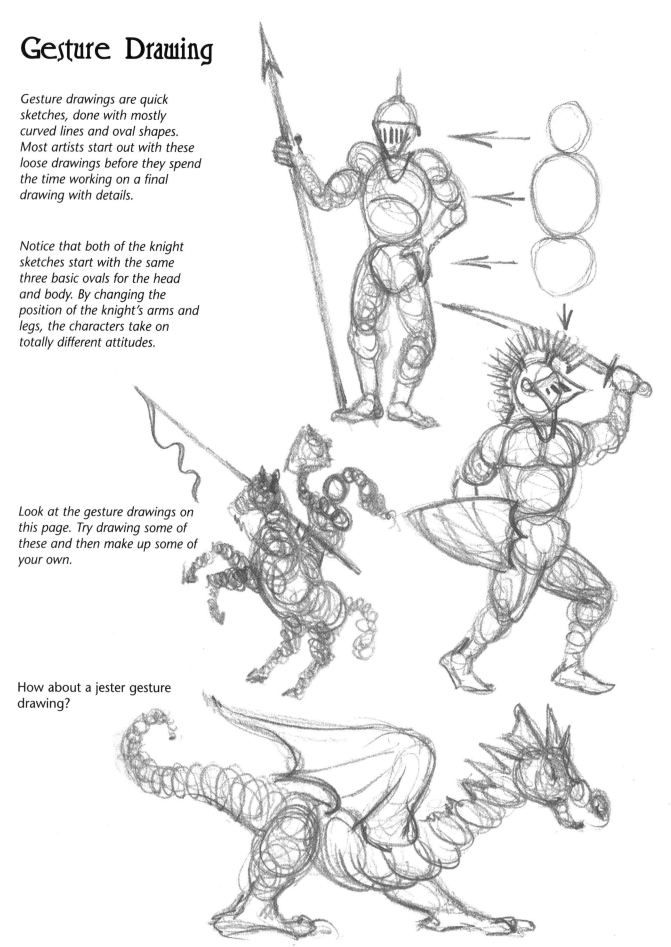

Chapter III

Dragons

Sea Serpent

Step 1

Sketch a small oval with an attached triangle on its end, to begin the tail of this mythical dragon.

To the right of the oval, draw a larger donut shape oval. Sketch the beginnings of the serpent's head and neck. Notice how many ovals, triangles and curved lines make up this first step.

Step 2

Round out and detail the fins on the sea serpent's head. Draw two bumps above the eye area. Add a large tongue. Sketch lines under the neck. Draw the tail and add spikes.

Draw some wiggly, wavy water lines.

Step 3

Look! A playful dragon? Draw the facial details. Don't forget the ear fins. Add spikes and lines to the donut-shaped body. Refine and round the stomach lines.

Step 4

You can use pencil shading to finish the sea serpent,

or...you can use a fine tip black marker to outline, and stipple (fine dots) to create shaded areas.

Stippling takes patience, but the effect is exciting!

Royal Dragon

Look at the symmetry in this drawing. One side mirrors the other. The dotted line shows the center of the design.

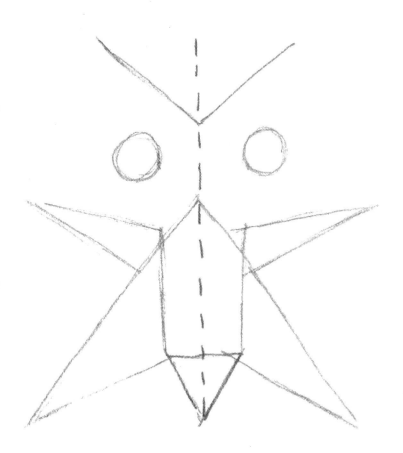

Step 1

Sketch triangles, lines and two ovals. Pay close attention to how these are spaced.

Compare step 1 to step 2. Leave enough room to add the lines and shapes you see in step 2.

Step 2

Sketch an arch across the V at the top of the head. This arch will give us the size of the dragon's crown. Sketch half ovals for the horn area. Add the ears and eyes. Add lines for the nose and nostrils.

Draw three more triangular shapes on either side of the face next to the eyes—remember symmetry!

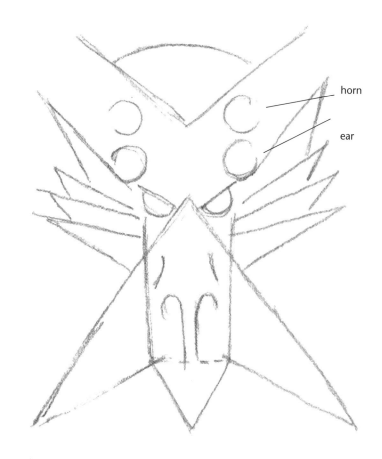

horn

ear

Step 3

Draw two curved V shapes to begin the crown on this majesty's head. Draw horns. Round and shape the lines of the dragon's face. How many triangular scales are on each side of the great creature's neck? Draw these.

Erase guide lines.

light

Step 4

See the light shining down on the dragon's head. Look at the shadows. See the fine details of shape, shading and texture. in this drawing.

Now, draw details. Starting at the top, round and shape the feather-like crown. Detail and refine the head and facial features. Draw circle textures on the face and neck. Round and shape the scales. Add sharp, jagged teeth.

Shade the royal dragon.

The Crowned Dragon

Step 1

Sketch an oval for the head and a larger oval for the body. Draw two curved lines for the neck. Sketch rods (lines) and joints (ovals) for the arms and legs. Add two curved lines for the tail.

Step 2

Outline and shape the arms. Add claws for the hands. Outline and shape the legs. Sketch ovals for the dragon's toes.

Erase the rods and joints guide lines.

Step 3

Look carefully at this dragon!

Sketch two flap shapes for the crown. Shape the head with an open mouth. Add the eye, ear and nostril. Draw a row of spiked fins along the back. Sketch lines under the throat, neck and stomach sections.

Draw the feet and claws.

Erase guide lines.

Look at your drawing!

Are any parts too large? Too small? If parts appear out of proportion, correct them before continuing!

Step 4

If you choose to stop at step 3, your drawing will look very dragon-like.

However, when you add more details, you can make your dragon AWESOME!

Use your imagination!

Spike the flaps. Shape the head, jaw and dorsal fins for more realism! Add jagged teeth. Shape and round the body lines. Add excitement with a unique pattern.

AWESOME Crowned Dragon!

Proud Papa

Step 1

Sketch a tilted oval for the head. Sketch an oval for the body, and a smaller one inside it for the leg. Notice how they are tilted a different way. Connect the head and the body with two curved lines.

Sketch a partial oval for the second leg. Draw a long, curved line for the tail. Draw another oval on the ground for the dragon egg.

Step 2

Add three fins to top of the head. Sketch in rods and joints for the arms. Add curved lines for claws. Sketch two curved lines to shape the neck and stomach. Draw legs and feet. Add another curved line to form the tail.

Oops…the egg is moving.

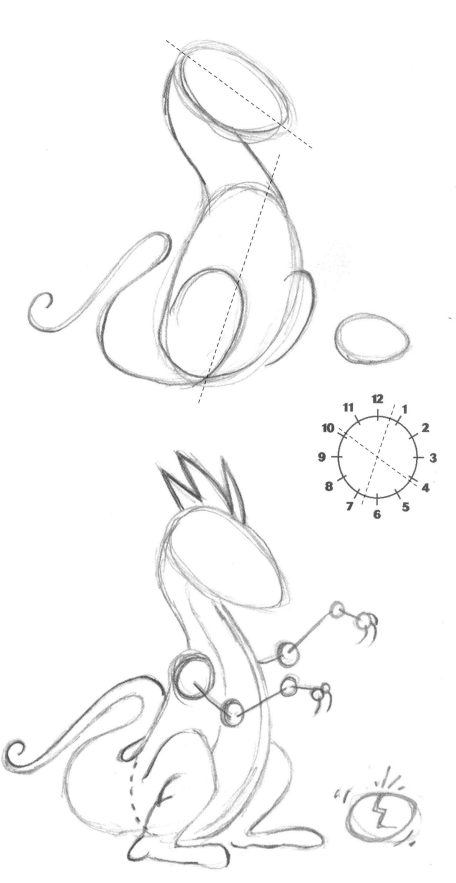

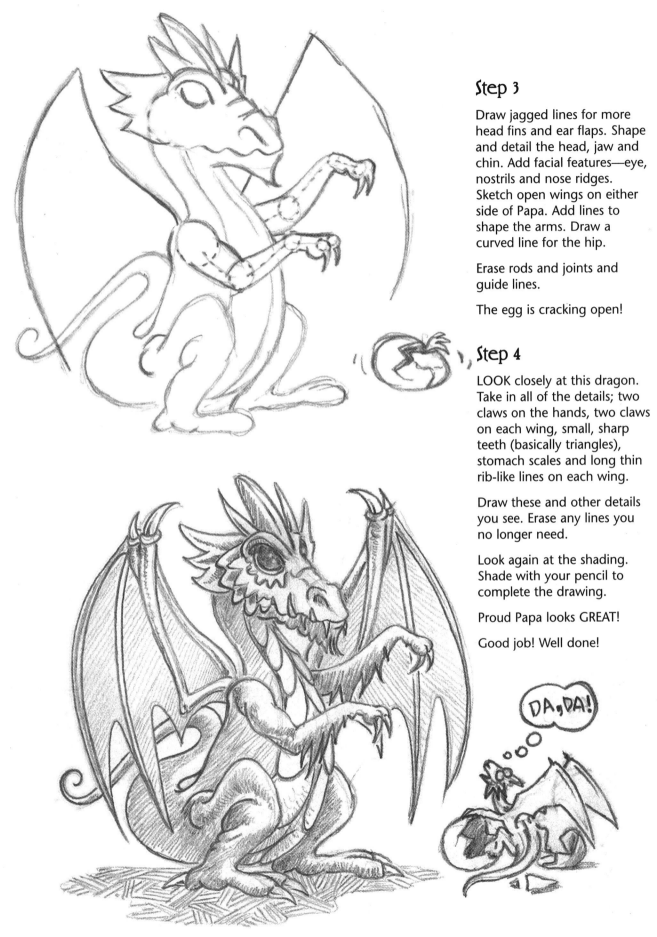

Step 3

Draw jagged lines for more head fins and ear flaps. Shape and detail the head, jaw and chin. Add facial features—eye, nostrils and nose ridges. Sketch open wings on either side of Papa. Add lines to shape the arms. Draw a curved line for the hip.

Erase rods and joints and guide lines.

The egg is cracking open!

Step 4

LOOK closely at this dragon. Take in all of the details; two claws on the hands, two claws on each wing, small, sharp teeth (basically triangles), stomach scales and long thin rib-like lines on each wing.

Draw these and other details you see. Erase any lines you no longer need.

Look again at the shading. Shade with your pencil to complete the drawing.

Proud Papa looks GREAT!

Good job! Well done!

DA, DA!

The Winged Menace

Step 1

Sketch a small oval for the head, and a larger oval for the body. Note the tilt of each.

Sketch two more ovals for the base of the neck. Add two curved lines for the neck.

Sketch another oval for the hip.

Draw the tail.

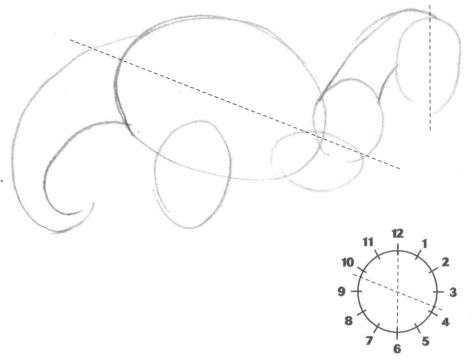

Step 2

Sketch the wings.

Draw two lines to form the mouth opening.

Sketch rods and joints for the arms and legs.

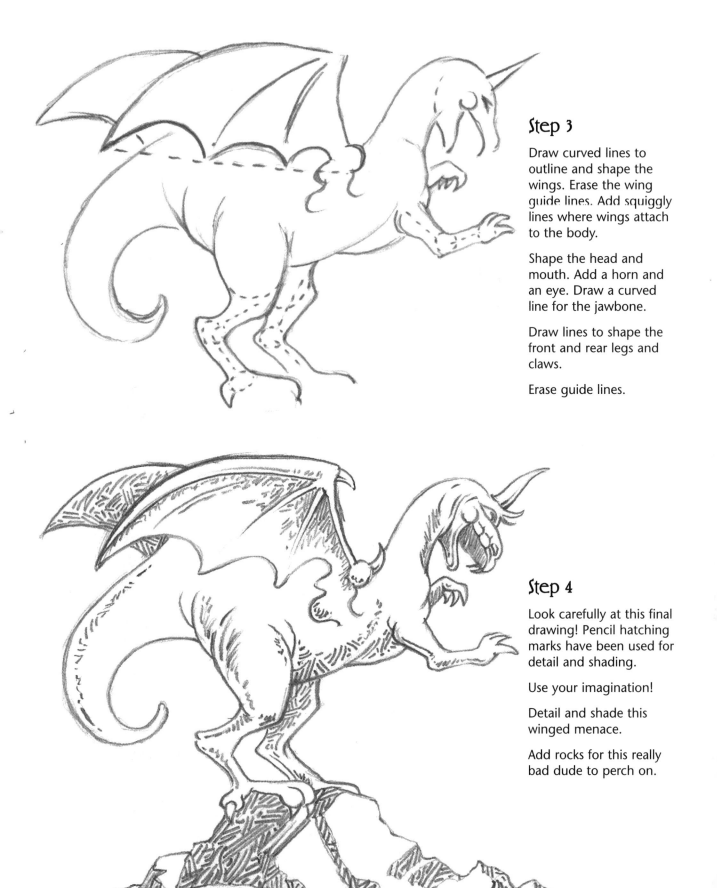

Step 3

Draw curved lines to outline and shape the wings. Erase the wing guide lines. Add squiggly lines where wings attach to the body.

Shape the head and mouth. Add a horn and an eye. Draw a curved line for the jawbone.

Draw lines to shape the front and rear legs and claws.

Erase guide lines.

Step 4

Look carefully at this final drawing! Pencil hatching marks have been used for detail and shading.

Use your imagination!

Detail and shade this winged menace.

Add rocks for this really bad dude to perch on.

Cartoon Dragon

Before you start, look carefully at the final drawing to see the basic shapes.

Step 1

Carefully draw the three curved lines.

Step 2

Draw an oval for the head. Shape the neck by drawing another curved line. Sketch ovals and lines to form the beginnings of the legs. Draw another curved line to shape the tail.

Step 3

Sketch four triangles for the wings. Sketch two lines for the opening of the mouth. Finish drawing the legs and feet. Add toes. Sketch lines on the stomach.

Step 4

Shape this happy dragon's head. Draw facial features. Round out and detail the body, tail and wings. Shape and round the stomach and neck lines.

Erase guide lines.

Finish your drawing with simple pencil line shading.

Tail   Neck

Chapter IV

Castles

Castles in Perspective

All the castles in this book begin with a horizon line (line across the middle of the paper) and a vanishing point, at each end of the horizon line.

Vanishing point

Horizon line

Vanishing point

Step 1

Sketch the horizon line and two x's for the vanishing points. Add a vertical line for the closest corner of the castle.

Sketch them all SUPER lightly!

Step 2

Draw two vertical lines for the far left and

right corners of the walls. Connect the walls by drawing two lines (top and bottom) that slant toward the left and right vanishing points.

Step 3

Draw lines for a second story. Draw towers with cone shaped roofs. Draw an arch and a drawbridge. Add details—a banner, brickwork, windows.

A moat?

Use your imagination to finish the drawing.

Notice all the lines that line up with the vanishing points!

Island Castle

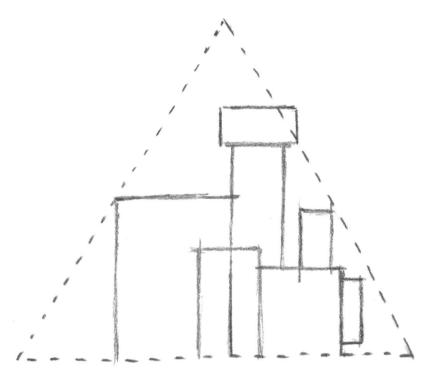

Step 1

Begin this drawing by sketching a very light triangle on your paper, represented here by a dotted line. Within the triangle, sketch squares and rectangles. These will become the major walls and towers of the castle. Notice how the corners of some of these basic shapes touch the sides of the triangle.

Step 2

Add a few small half oval shapes for rocks. Add a triangular shape on the far left wall. This structure is called a buttress. It helps support large castle and cathedral walls. Draw the buttress on the other side. Draw more towers. Add triangles for cone shaped peaks. Draw lines for the base of the twin turrets.

Look!

When drawing the triangular tower cones, curve them upward in the middle of their bases, like these.

Step 3

Add the twin turrets. Draw a peaked roof behind them. To make your castle seem more like an island castle, add an arch in the buttress.

Next draw a vertical line between the front gate towers for the main entrance. Look carefully at the ramp descending from the main entrance. Draw the ramp.

No castle is worth its salt without crenelations (indentations). Add some to the castle walls.

Step 4

Add crenelations to the big tower and the twin towers. Draw windows. Add a rectangular roof on the structure that is just inside the entrance. Make the peaks on the tower roofs more pointed.

Notice how the horizon line shows through the buttress arch of the castle. This gives the drawing more depth. Draw the horizon line.

Drawing Tips

As you sketch the tower and turrets, pretend they are cardboard paper rolls with tuna cans as tops! Better yet...Raid your kitchen cabinets for cans, find some paper towel or toilet paper rolls. Arrange these with some cardboard boxes, and VOILA! you have a model castle to draw from. Rearrange it and draw it over and over again!

Step 5

Make your castle more and more believable by adding simple details like random brickwork on towers and walls. Draw shingle designs on roof peaks. Shade in using pencil hatching. Create a dramatic mood by adding a large moon and soaring sea gulls!

Castle with Moat

Step 1

Start this castle by sketching the horizon line with a vanishing point at each end. Draw a vertical (up and down) line to represent the closest corner of the castle walls.

Step 2

Draw additional vertical lines at each side of the castle to show where the castle ends. Be aware that the horizontal lines of the building always line up with the vanishing points, at either side of the paper.

Using the same two vanishing points and your ruler, draw lines for the top and bottom of the walls. Add a second story.

Draw an arched entrance. Again using the vanishing points and your ruler, draw a draw bridge coming from the entrance.

Step 3

Draw towers at each corner. Notice how the sides of the towers slant inward to create a sense of vertical perspective.

Draw wavy, curved lines to begin the moat.

Step 4

To create more height, draw additional towers on the second story. Add turrets to the top of the corner towers. Draw a cone shape for the tower peak. Add windows, noting how they slant toward the vanishing point.

Draw wavy lines and drop-offs at the edge of the island.

Step 5

Add cone peaks to the back towers. Place battlement walls on top of the second story and the corner towers.

Draw a zigzag pattern on tower peaks and add randomly placed brickwork, for additional realism. Add more windows.

Look carefully at the wavy, squiggly lines that create the moat and water. Draw these. Detail the iron gate. Add the ropes to secure the bridge.

Draw Medieval Fantasies 41

More Castle Ideas

Use your imagination!

Have fun playing with different castle ideas.

What would an *ice castle* look like?

What's the most remote, inaccessible place you can imagine for a castle?

If you were a bird—flying by, looking down on a castle— what would you see?

Chapter V
Heroes and Villains

16th Century Armor

Here are the basic parts of Medieval armor. It is important to remember what part goes where. If you remember the placement of each part, it will make creating characters and their armor easier.

A Crest
 ornament on a helmet

B Visor
 piece to protect the face

C Gorget
 armor for the neck

D Breastplate
 protection for front of body

E Tasset
 armor for the hips

F Chain Mail
 flexible metal links

G Cuisse
 plate to protect the thighs

H Poleyn
 plate knee guards

I Greave
 below the knee protection

J Sabaton
 broad toed foot armor

K Pauldron
 shoulder cop

L Rerebrace
 above the elbow protection

M Elbow Cop
 elbow guard

N Gauntlet
 hand armor

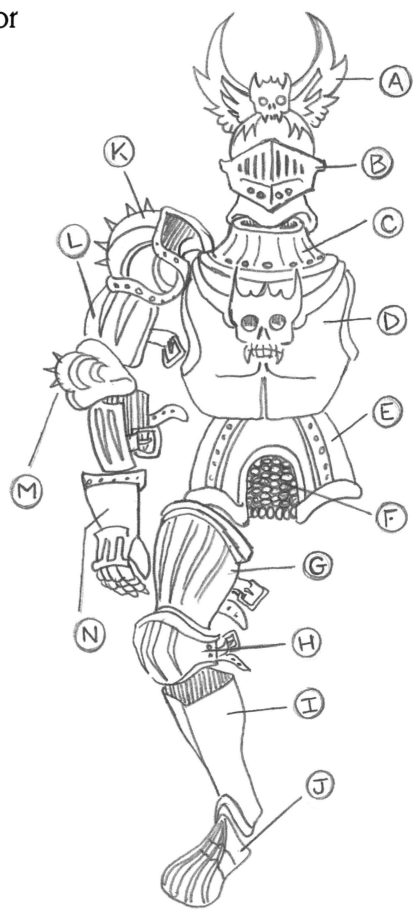

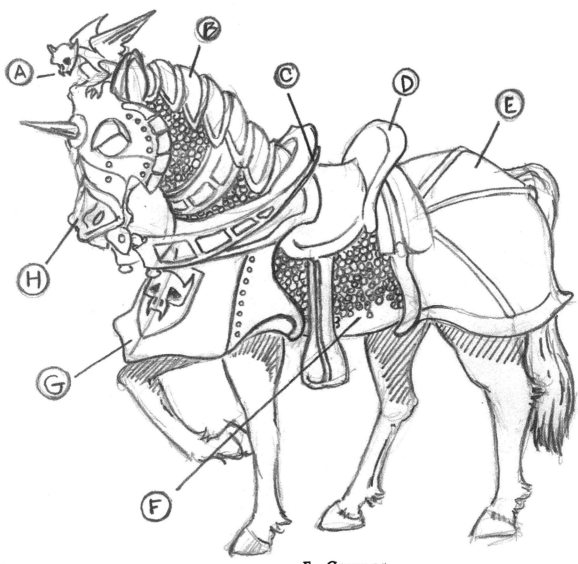

A Crest
usually matches the symbol which appears on the knight's helmet crest and shield

B Crinet
a series of short, sharp feather-like bends that form protective armor

C Reins
straps to control horse's movement

D Saddle
padded seat for a horse's rider

E Crupper
a leather, cloth or armor piece that wraps around the tail and is buckled to the saddle

F Flanchards
protection for the horse's side and belly—sometimes plate, sometimes chain mail

G Peytral
armor for a horse's chest

H Chanfron
protective head covering

Princess Warrior

Step 1

Look carefully at the tilt of ovals, and the direction each line runs. Use the clock face as a reference.

Lightly sketch ovals for the head, shoulder, torso, and pelvis. Sketch the rods and joints for the arm and legs.

Sketch an oval, beneath the hand oval, for the warrior's right hand. Sketch a straight line and a long, curved line for the beginning of her sword.

Step 2

Draw the face profile. Add the eye. Draw a line, up from the forehead, to begin the helmet. Add a backward 3 for the top. Shape the arm and legs. Add feet and hands. Draw the breast plate and skirt. Draw wavy lines for the start of her hair, and a flap for the helmet.

The Princess could be holding a club, a spear, a torch or almost anything. I gave her a sword. Draw lines to shape the sword and handle.

Erase all guide lines except the one directly under her left hand (this will become her right hand in step 3).

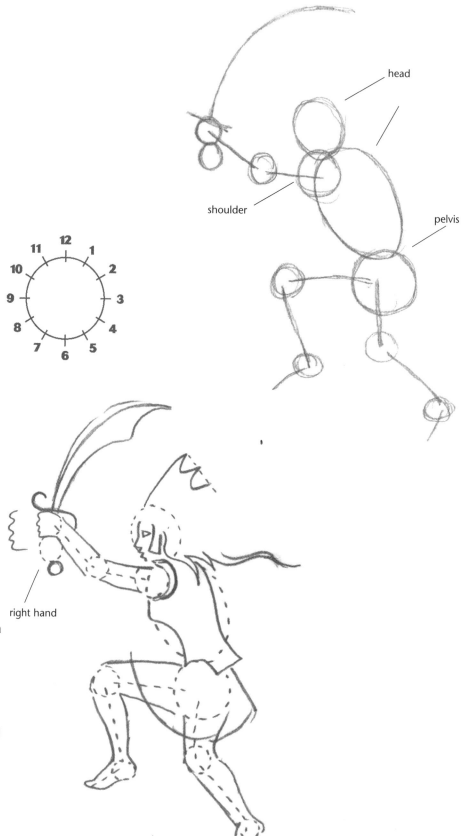

Step 3

Now things are really beginning to shape up! Draw more wavy lines for her hair. Add curved lines for the helmet crest. Draw her right arm, hand and fingers. Draw lines for gloves, and jagged lines for the glove's fringe.

Draw skirt sections. Add lines on knee area for poleyns (knee protection). Draw lines for foot coverings (sabatons).

Step 4

Now, for the details! Let's start with the head. Draw the small dragon crest. On the pauldrons (shoulders) draw layered petal shapes. Draw and shape the breast plate. Add straps.

Detail the skirt. Detail the poleyns, with the same small dragon design used on the crest of the helmet. Add simple line details to the sabatons.

Look

See the shapes! Together, all these details may seem a bit overwhelming, but if you really look, they are quite simple. The lines on the skirt and sabatons are just that! LINES! The straps on the breastplate, LINES! The fringe under the glove, jagged LINES! Draw step by step and keep it simple!

Dragon Swan

Step 1

Set up this figure by sketching light ovals, circles, rectangles and triangles. As always, pencil basic shapes lightly so they can easily be erased, if need be!

Use the clock face, for reference, to check that your ovals are correctly tilted and lines run in the right directions.

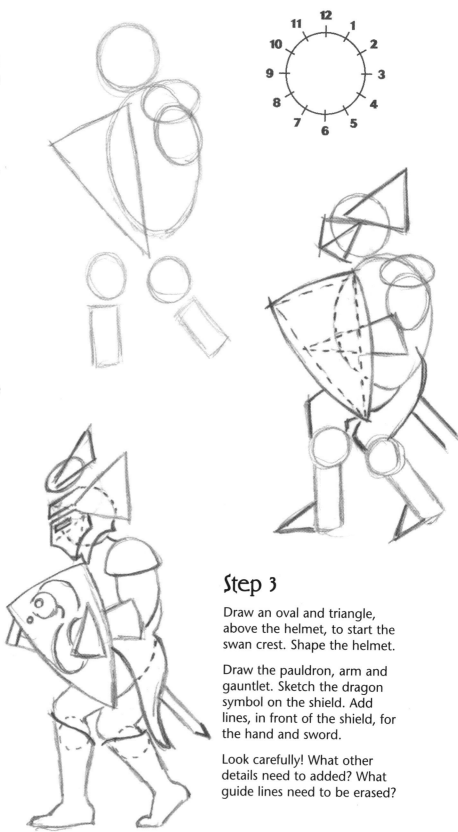

Step 2

Sketch three triangles to begin the helmet. (Compare their sizes.)

Shape the shield. Sketch a triangle for the arm holding the shield.

Shape the legs. Add a triangle for each foot. Draw two lines, below the right hip, to begin the sheath for the sword.

Erase guide lines.

Step 3

Draw an oval and triangle, above the helmet, to start the swan crest. Shape the helmet.

Draw the pauldron, arm and gauntlet. Sketch the dragon symbol on the shield. Add lines, in front of the shield, for the hand and sword.

Look carefully! What other details need to added? What guide lines need to be erased?

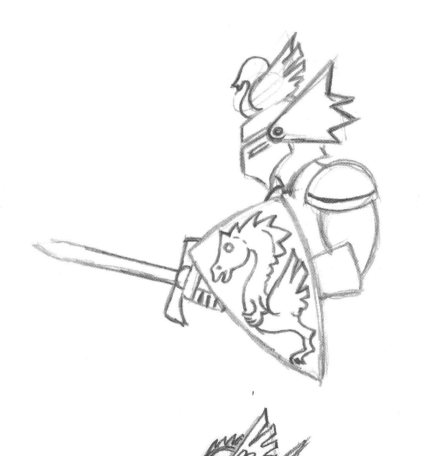

Step 4

Let's add more details....

Take your time. Do one detail at a time!

Shape the swan crest.

Draw jagged lines to shape the fin on the knight's helmet.

Draw the sword. Add lines to form the fingers and thumb holding the sword.

Finish the dragon design on the shield.

Step 5

Finish your drawing using pencil to add more details and to shade.

Draw a pattern on his cloak, vent holes on his visor, spikes on his pauldron (uh, what was that again? Oh, right, his shoulder. See page 44). How about some engraved designs on his boots and sheath?

Don't forget his chain mail. Now, he's flexible and ready to battle!

The Nomad

Before you begin to draw the nomad, look carefully at the placement and tilt of ovals, joints and rods.

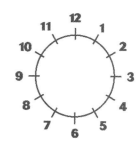

Step 1

Sketch the ovals, rods and joints for the nomad's head, body and arms.

Step 2

Add the facial features. Draw jagged, wavy lines for hair. Shape chest and body. Add lines for the pelvis area.

Sketch the rods and joints for the legs.

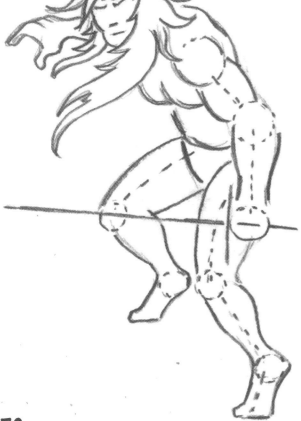

Step 3

Draw the nomad's right hand.

Outline and shape the body, left arm and legs.

Erase guide lines.

Draw lines for the sword.

Step 4

Use pencil to shade and detail the nomad's intense face.

Shade and sharpen lines to give a sense of muscular form to his body.

Draw jagged lines to add fur like texture to his loincloth.

Draw the sword.

Look!

Once you have the basics of a figure on paper, you can totally change its look with the details you add!

NOW this Nomad character really has an axe to grind! He also sports a helmet and shield, with matching symbols on both (which was customary in medieval times). Chain mail covers his thighs.

Notice how the cast shadow adds realism and depth.

By the way, did you know that Nomad spelled backwards is DAMON?

Dragon Slayer

Step 1

Look at this sketch! Notice the tilt of each oval, rod and joint.

Now, sketch ovals for the horse's head, neck, body and rump.

Sketch rods and joints for the legs.

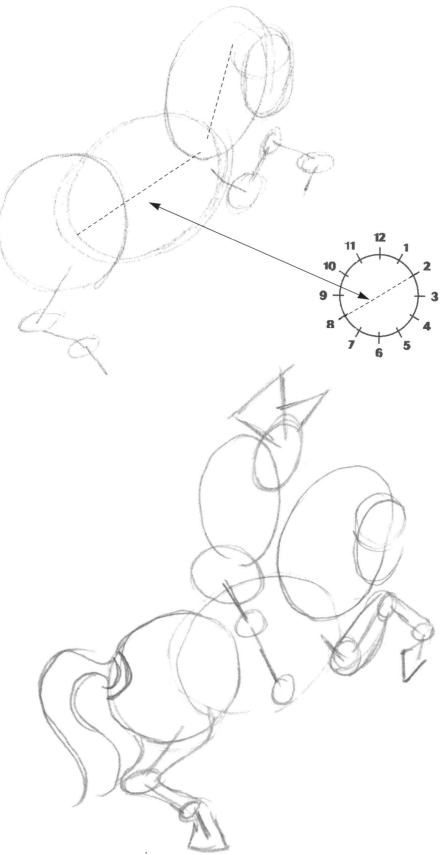

Step 2

Sketch ovals for the knight's body and head. Sketch two triangle shapes for the helmet. Sketch rods and joints for the knight's leg.

Draw two curved lines for the horse's tail, and two curved lines for the ring on the crupper (see page 45 for parts of horse armor).

Outline and shape the horse's legs. Add hooves.

Step 3

Sketch the rods and joints for the knight's right arm and lance handle. Draw a long line for the lance. Add the visor and shield. Shape the knight's leg and foot.

Sketch rods and joints for the horse's inside legs. Draw zigzag lines for the reins and crupper. Shape the horse's head and neck. Draw the ear, eye and nostril.

Erase guide lines you no longer need.

Step 4

Shape the knight's visor fins. Draw the arm and lance. Add jagged lines to the elbow, for the rerebrace. Add breast plate lines.

Sketch the outline of the horse's mane. Draw ovals and lines for the horse's bridle. Shape inside legs and hooves. Draw the saddle, and saddle cinch. Add lines for a fuller tail.

Erase guide lines.

Saddle cinch

Step 5

Now for some dragon slayer details....

Create a wild mane for the horse! Detail the knight's visor and armor. Design a crest for the shield. Draw a pattern on the horse's crupper. Shade horse and rider and add other details you see.

Use your imagination!

Draw a dragon slaying scene!

Chapter VI
Texture and Pattern

Basic shading and line techniques can add simulated texture, depth and excitement to your drawings....

Row 1

Horizontal lines shows direction and stability. Add vertical lines for cross hatch shading. Add diagonal lines over those for even darker shaded areas! See illustration, page 20.

Row 2

To create a marble or rock surface: start by sketching very lightly shaded grays—then gradually add darker shading. This technique is used on page 54.

Row 3

A repeating pattern suggests scales or skin. Squares 2 and 3 show patterns useful for dragon skin. This technique is used on page 29.

Row 4

Square 1 shows how to add texture to shadow areas. See illustration, page 51.The square 2 design suggests flames. Square 3 suggests bubbles, fish eggs, or an underwater scene. Try them in your drawings!

Row 5

I love DOTS! Use a fine tip black marker for this technique, called stippling. It takes time... but is well worth it! Examples of stippling are all through this book. The last two squares use thick and thin line design—a bold background idea for one of your drawings?

Here are more ideas for patterns and textures that I have used throughout this book, and which you might find useful in your drawing.

Row 1

This random dot and circle can add excitement and variety to the background—try it!

Row 2

I used crosshatching in many of my drawing—take a moment to flip through this book and find other examples of it.

Row 3

Vary the shape and spacing of stones to make your castle walls more interesting and realistic.

Row 4

Patterns can add a lot of interest to your drawings! Notice the patterns here: bricks across the otherwise plain wall, and the pattern of the diagonal drawbridge hoist chain. Look for ways to put patterns in your drawing.

Row 5

Shading helps create a sense of form, but scales. on a dragon, make it jump out at you! Notice that these scales are nothing more than the letter u repeated over and over!

These circles illustrate four different patterns or techniques. Can you find these patterns in the drawing below? Can you see ways to use them in your drawings?

Chapter VII

Putting It All Together

Onward!

Step 1

Begin this drawing by sketching ovals for the head, neck and body of the horse. Sketch the rods and joints for the legs.

Check the clock face to determine which direction to draw lines, or how to tilt ovals.

By now this should be getting easier for you!

Step 2

Outline the horse's body. Draw curved lines under the stomach area to begin the crupper. Shape legs. Add a flowing tail.

Sketch an oval for the rider's head. Sketch the rods and joints for his arm and leg. Sketch the shield. Draw a long line for the lance, and an oval for the handle. Draw curved lines for the front and back of the saddle.

What other lines do you see that you need to add or erase at this stage of the drawing? Add or subtract these.

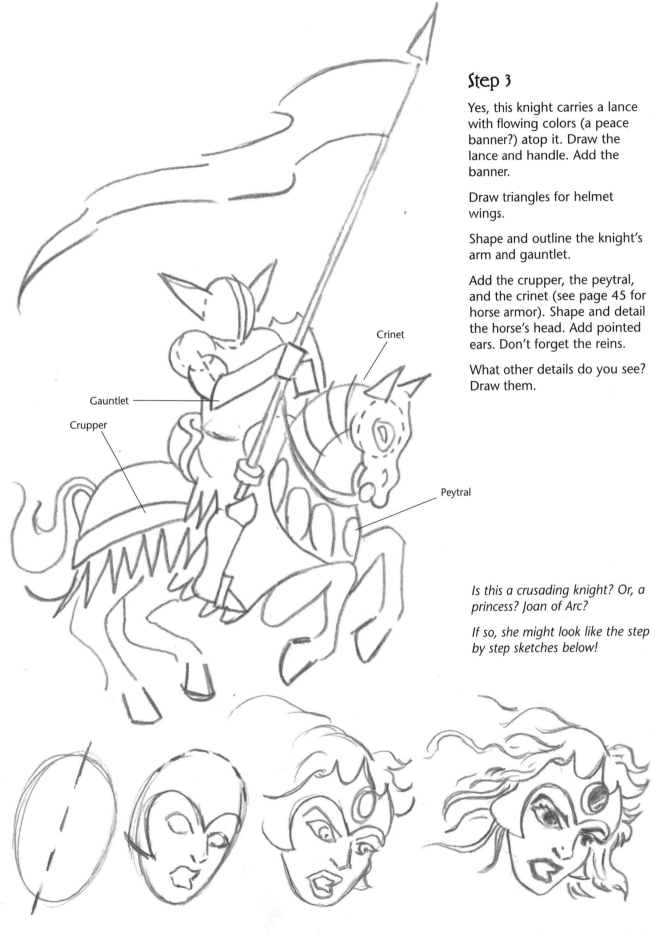

Step 3

Yes, this knight carries a lance with flowing colors (a peace banner?) atop it. Draw the lance and handle. Add the banner.

Draw triangles for helmet wings.

Shape and outline the knight's arm and gauntlet.

Add the crupper, the peytral, and the crinet (see page 45 for horse armor). Shape and detail the horse's head. Add pointed ears. Don't forget the reins.

What other details do you see? Draw them.

Is this a crusading knight? Or, a princess? Joan of Arc?

If so, she might look like the step by step sketches below!

Crinet

Gauntlet

Crupper

Peytral

Step 4

Let's add more details....

Finish the banner and lance. Detail the shield. Shape and detail the helmet. Add plumes to the wings. Add spikes to the pauldrons. Detail the gauntlet. Design and detail the crupper. Add chain mail dots to protect the flank area of the horse. Finish the crinet.

Shade horse and rider and add other details you see.

Step 5

And now, let's put it all together in an action scene.

Use your imagination!

Turn back to page 59 to view my action scene of Joan of Arc moving onward.

Pauldron

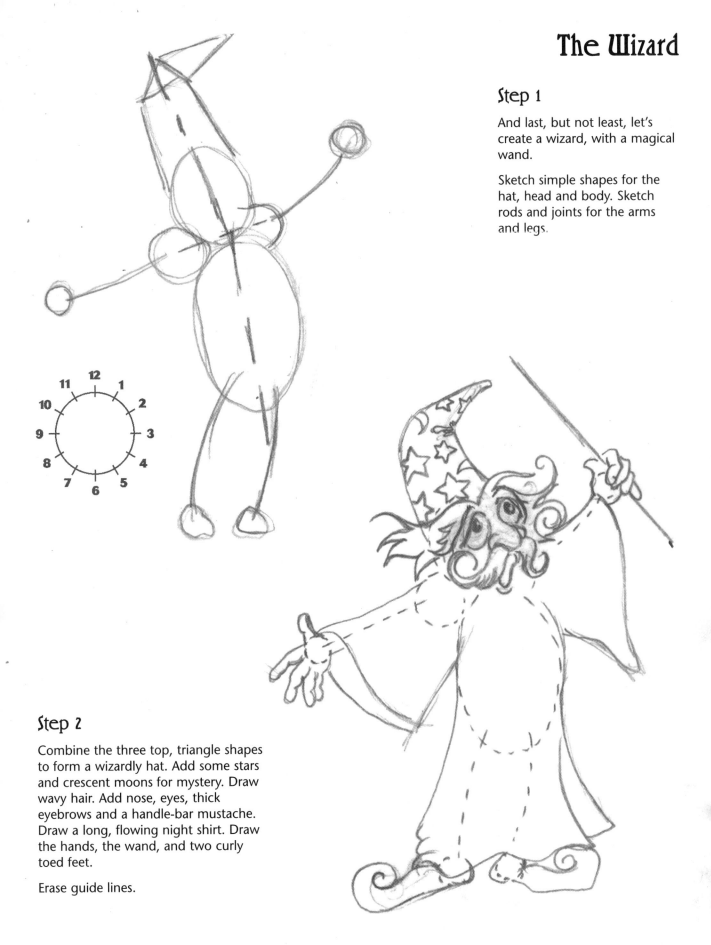

The Wizard

Step 1

And last, but not least, let's create a wizard, with a magical wand.

Sketch simple shapes for the hat, head and body. Sketch rods and joints for the arms and legs.

Step 2

Combine the three top, triangle shapes to form a wizardly hat. Add some stars and crescent moons for mystery. Draw wavy hair. Add nose, eyes, thick eyebrows and a handle-bar mustache. Draw a long, flowing night shirt. Draw the hands, the wand, and two curly toed feet.

Erase guide lines.

STOP!

Look closely at this drawing!

Did the wizard create it with one wave of his magical wand?

Step 3

Let's ask Merlin…

How did he do it? Will he share the secret? Pretty please?

Postscript

It's easy! Really! Just…

1. LOOK!

2. Sketch super lightly!

3. Use your imagination!

4. Practice, Practice, Practice!

and, like magic, you will get better and better!

And, if you ever need advice, or encouragement on a drawing…. **Ask any wizard**— an artist, a teacher, a friend— they've always got good ideas!

GET OFF MY TAIL, BUSTER!

Request a current brochure from
Peel Productions, Inc.
PO Box 546, Columbus NC 28722
Find samples from other books on the web at

www.drawbooks.com